Shakespeare
for
LAWYERS

A Practical Guide to
Quoting the Bard

Shakespeare
for
LAWYERS

A PRACTICAL GUIDE TO QUOTING THE BARD

MARGARET GRAHAM TEBO

AMERICAN BAR ASSOCIATION
Defending Liberty
Pursuing Justice

Cover design by ABA Publishing.

Cover and internal photo credit © istockphoto.com/claudiodivizia.

Printed in the United States of America

14 13 12 11 10   5 4 3 2

Library of Congress Cataloging-in-Publication Data

Tebo, Margaret Graham.
  Shakespeare for lawyers : A practical guide to quoting the bard / Margaret Graham Tebo.
   p. cm.
  ISBN 978-1-60442-836-0
  1. Shakespeare, William, 1564–1616—Criticism and interpretation. 2. Shakespeare, William, 1564–1616—Quotations. 3. Shakespeare, William, 1564–1616—Knowledge—Law. 4. Law in literature. 5. Quotations, English. I. Title.
  PR3028.T43 2010
  822.3'3—dc22

                                                                            2010004526

Discounts are available for books ordered in bulk. Special consideration is given to state bars, CLE programs, and other bar-related organizations. Inquire at Book Publishing, ABA Publishing, American Bar Association, 321 North Clark Street, Chicago, Illinois 60654-7598.

www.ababooks.org

Dedication

For my mother, Peggy Scharr Tebo
Who read to me before I could speak
Fostering a passion for reading and writing
that set my life's path
And whose love and encouragement
are my lifelong inspiration

Contents

Acknowledgments

As with any such undertaking, this book would not have been possible without a whole lot of help.

First, William Shakespeare, without whom not only this book but much of Western literature would not exist.

To every English teacher I ever had, all of whom taught me to love words unabashedly and to read the best wordsmiths for inspiration: Thank you.

And to every editor I've ever had who taught me to write tighter and challenged me to be precise but never dry: Thank you.

Specifically, I must thank ABA Publishing's Erin Nevius, the editor who asked me if I was interested in this project after she thought it up. I think my immediate reply was something like, *"Um, YEAH!"* Thanks for your patience, your good humor, and your insights. Your patience most of all. I know I tried it mightily.

Also to the proofreader, Kate Doman, whose fine catches saved me from major embarrassment when some of the sources of the quotes herein got garbled in translation. You are an underrated gem!

Thanks to my "boss" (even though she hates that term) Nancy Day, chair of the Journalism Department at Columbia College Chicago, and to all of my colleagues there for the mentoring and the opportunities to join in the great adventure of teaching undergraduates to think critically and write journalistically.

Thanks to the ladies of my writing group, the Dirty Dozen Chicago, for taking me in, propping me up, and motivating me with countless hours of educational and fun conversation.

To my family, friends, and colleagues through the years who always read my stuff and tell me it's good, whether or not that's true.

And finally, to my best girl, Elise Pullen. You are my rock, my comforter and my inspiration.

Prologue

The connection between the law and Shakespeare seems so obvious as to be almost cliché. Lawyers are connoisseurs of the well-turned phrase, and none was a better wordsmith of English than the Bard.

Indeed, it is lawyers who are most often at the wrong end of lay people's feeble attempts to connect Shakespeare and our noble profession: Is there an attorney alive who has never heard, "The first thing we do, let's kill all the lawyers"? Of course, what most people fail to recognize is that phrase was uttered with irony in *King Henry VI* (not, as many mistakenly believe, in *Hamlet* or *Macbeth*). The phrase was meant to be rhetorical—as if a modern-day politician said that the way to fix the education system is to eliminate public schools. Few would take this seriously, and they would certainly not be the mainstream. And so it is with Shakespeare and lawyers.

But we in the profession love to quote him too. In these pages you will find his most famous quotes, as well as many that are less well-known but which resonate strongly when viewed through the particular prism of the legal profession.

Take this book with you as you wait your turn at a long court call, or turn to it for a break in the middle of brief writing. You can't help but be inspired.

And when your career is finished, may these words
from King Henry VIII be applied to you:

He was a scholar, and a ripe and good one;
Exceeding wise, fair-spoken and persuading;
Lofty and sour to them that lov'd him not;
But to those men that sought him, sweet as summer.

—Margaret Graham Tebo
November 2009

Chapter One
A Rhapsody of Words

Bid me discourse,
I will enchant thine ear.

—Venus and Adonis

Lawyers love a well-turned phrase. In law school, they teach that there are two kinds of lawyers: litigators and transactional attorneys. But once you're out in the world practicing, you find many more distinctions—including lawyers who dread having to put pen to paper and those who love all things literary, even the often rote task of brief writing.

This latter group's comprehensive knowledge of grammar, punctuation, and precise prepositional usage is rivaled only by English teachers and librarians. They can argue for hours over the proper use of the semi-colon, and there's nary a one who doesn't have at least a dozen favorite quotations ready to be tossed off at the slightest opportunity.

Here, then, are a few fresh gems.

He draweth out the thread of verbosity
finer than the staple of his argument.

— Love's Labour's Lost

What it means: He's "all fluff, no stuff." That is, he talks and talks, but in the end his argument is weak.

How to use it: When your opponent is talking in circles, and attempting to sound smart and reasonable, but you know his argument is just hot air.

Well roared, Lion.

—A Midsummer Night's Dream

What it means: There could be several meanings here. It can be read as a true compliment that a speaker has stated his case strongly, or it could be sarcastic, used to highlight the fact that what was said was more loud than substantive.

How to use it: To compliment co- or opposing counsel on a good argument, or to point out the bullying nature of what was said, and the fact that being the loudest doesn't mean one has the strongest argument.

> No epilogue, I pray you,
> for your play needs no excuse. Never excuse.

> — *A Midsummer Night's Dream*

What it means: When you have said what you needed to say, stop talking. Don't try to further explain or apologize. Just let the facts speak for themselves.

How to use it: When you or your client are tempted to keep talking, keep explaining, keep trying to convince someone of something. Remind yourself or the client to just let stand the strong argument already made.

I *will* make thee think thy *swan* a crow.

— Romeo and Juliet

What it means: I can convince you that the thing you think is so great is simply ordinary, or perhaps even bad.

How to use it: When you need to explain to someone why something that appears to be wonderful really isn't. Perhaps there's a development in the case that at first blush seems to be a victory for your side, but on further review raises new problems.

*Thank me no thankings,
Nor proud me no prouds.*

— Romeo and Juliet

What it means: Don't thank me; don't tell me you're proud of me. What I have done isn't worthy of praise. It was just something that had to be done.

How to use it: When you have done something you wish you didn't have to do, such as impeached a witness in a manner that scored the legal point you needed, but left the witness deflated and perhaps humiliated. Alternately, you can use it to mean don't thank me yet. We have scored, but the game isn't over.

A *good mouth-filling oath*.

— Henry IV

What it means: This can be read sarcastically, as in "If he swore it, then it must be true."

How to use it: To impeach a witness or point out the weakness of your opponent's assertion; for example, "Oh, well, if he says he didn't lie, then we must, of course believe him. Unless, of course, he's lying again now."

The better part of valor is discretion.

— Henry IV

What it means: It is important to keep others' confidences, and not to gossip about others' private business.

How to use it: To assure a client that what he tells you is confidential. You could also use it to remind staff of the need for keeping client confidences, or as your answer when someone seeks your counsel as to whether to reveal something he or she knows. Note that this last is only true where the telling of the secret is discretionary. Of course this line should not be used as an excuse to fail to reveal something that the law or court rules mandate must be revealed.

13

Harp not on that string.

— Richard III

What it means: In the most literal legal sense, this could be taken to mean the same thing as the objection "Asked and answered." In a broader sense, it means that everyone present has heard this before.

How to use it: When someone keeps returning to the same theme, such as an opponent who continues to raise the same point again and again. You can also use it when your opponent is about to strike a low blow, such as bringing up a sensitive issue that is designed to embarrass your client, but is not relevant to the proceedings at hand. Use this phrase as a way of saying "Don't go there."

I am not in the giving vein today.

— Richard III

What it means: I am not in the mood to negotiate. We have a strong argument, and we are not of a mind to give concessions when we don't need to.

How to use it: When an opponent is asking for too much in a negotiation. This could also be used by a judge who is being asked for more mercy than the situation might warrant.

I am Sir Oracle,
And when I ope my lips, let no dog bark!

— The Merchant of Venice

What it means: I am so smart! People listen to me because I am full of wisdom. This could be an expression of joy, similar to Leonardo DiCaprio's exuberant "I'm the king of the world!" as he stood on the bow of the Titanic (before the iceberg). Or it could be sarcastic—a means of calling out someone who thinks he is smarter than everyone else.

How to use it: As an expression of joy, such as to celebrate a big win. This should perhaps be limited to use among one's closest colleagues, family or friends, lest it come off as arrogant. Alternately, it can be used sarcastically to deride someone who is displaying an excess of arrogance.

The Devil can cite Scripture for his purpose.

— The Merchant of Venice

What it means: Don't let pretty words fool you. This speaker's intent is evil, despite the seeming rationality of the way he makes his argument.

How to use it: To counter an opposing counsel's argument; for example, "It all sounds so reasonable when he says it like that. But stop and think about what he's really advocating."

Here will be an old abusing of God's patience
and the King's English.

— The Merry Wives of Windsor

What it means: The upcoming speaker is about to make a long-winded, inarticulate speech.

How to use it: When someone is about to speak and you expect the speech to be long and circular and make little sense. This is especially useful when the speaker is about to attempt to defend the indefensible.

> Why, then, the world's mine oyster,
> With which sword I will open.

—The Merry Wives of Windsor

What it means: I can do anything. My whole life is ahead of me, and I have the tools to succeed.

How to use it: To congratulate a recent law school graduate, or a young associate who has just begun to prove himself. Or, perhaps, to remind yourself that you can do other things beyond what you're currently doing.

And ſheath'd their ſwords for lack of argument.

— Henry V

What it means: I can't argue with that.

How to use it: Perhaps you are expecting a tough negotiation, only to find that you and your opponent are in essential agreement. Alternately, use this to show that whatever was just said is the last and definitive word on a subject—that no reasonable person could disagree.

There's a skirmish of wit between them.

— *Much Ado about Nothing*

What it means: Two (or more) smart, knowledgeable, well-spoken people are trading rhetorical jabs.

How to use it: This could be used as an expression of resignation; that all speakers are making good points, but no one seems to be winning the argument. Or it could simply be used to describe the action as it unfolds—you're enjoying the back-and-forth while you wait to see what happens.

Abuse of greatness is what disjoins
Remorse from Power.

—Julius Caesar

What it means: Someone is abusing his or her position. Someone has mistaken his or her popularity as an excuse to circumvent proper procedures.

How to use it: To call out someone who, while perhaps justifiably respected, is using their authority improperly.

Friends, Romans, Countrymen, lend me your ears;
I come to bury Caesar, not to praise him.
The evil that men do lives after them,
The good is oft interred with their bones.

— Julius Caesar

What it means: Let's not forget that this person we're inclined to praise did some very bad things. The reverberations of his crimes continue.

How to use it: When someone is inclined to hold up as a positive example someone or something that is undeserving of such consideration. Perhaps someone is reviving an old idea that was set aside for a very good reason long ago.

Or perhaps someone is doing such a good job of defending one who did a terrible thing that the terrible thing, and the victims of it, nearly get lost in the hyperbole.

If you have tears,
prepare to shed them now.

— *Julius Caesar*

What it means: I am about to tell you a heartbreaking story.

How to use it: To prepare an audience to hear what you have to say when your story will be emotional. This could also be sardonic, as if to say, "I know that you're not going to have much sympathy when I tell you my tale of a bad guy wronged by his bad-guy associate, but hear me out."

For I *have* neither wit, nor words, nor worth,
Action, nor utterance, nor the power of speech,
To stir men's blood: I speak only right on.

— Julius Caesar

What it means: I cannot dazzle you with my great speaking skills, or any other showy examples of my side of the story. But I will tell you the simple truth.

How to use it: This is particularly useful when your opponent has all sorts of technology at his fingertips with which to dazzle the jury, and you have nothing to offer but "the truth."

What's the new news at the new court?

— *As You Like It*

What it means: What's up?

How to use it: As a friendly greeting. Best used when you expect there is, in fact, some news to report.

Well said: that was laid on with a trowel.

— As You Like It

What it means: You have certainly overstated your case.

How to use it: When your opponent makes a pitch, whether in negotiations or in court, that, while it has some value, is simply overwrought.

The "why" is as plain as the way to the parish church.

— As You Like It

What it means: The reason is obvious.

How to use it: When someone questions a motive, and you believe the question to be specious. For example: Lawyer A: "Why would my client kill his wife?" Lawyer B: "Why? Do I really need to point out that there was a life insurance policy for $2 million?"

Season your admiration for a while.

— Hamlet

What it means: Don't applaud now. You haven't heard the whole story yet.

How to use it: When the court seems moved by the tale told by your opposing counsel, such as in an opening argument. Alternatively, it could be read as "Don't thank me yet. It's not over."

Give it an understanding, but no tongue.

—Hamlet

What it means: Listen to this, but don't repeat it.

How to use it: I am entrusting you with a confidence. There's something you need to know, but you cannot tell anybody else.

Brevity is the soul of wit.

— Hamlet

What it means: Make what you have to say short and sweet and people will remember it better.

How to use it: To remind yourself, someone to whom you are giving advice, or your audience that it is often better to be brief and memorable than long-winded and boring.

More matter, with less art.

— Hamlet

What it means: More substance, less decoration. More stuff, less fluff.

How to use it: As a reminder that flowery language will take you only so far, but evidence and example will win the day.

Find out the cause of this effect,
Or rather say, the cause of this defect,
For this effect defective comes by cause.

— Hamlet

What it means: Something happened, and something caused it to happen. Someone is responsible.

How to use it: This would be an effective response to an opponent who contends that some occurrence was by happenstance, when your argument is that negligence or some other human error caused the problem.

35

Sometimes we are devils to ourselves
When we will tempt the frailty of our powers,
Presuming their changeful potency.

— Troilus and Cressida

What it means: Don't bite off more than you can chew.

How to use it: As a tempering reminder that you cannot accomplish everything you'd like to in one move. Your whole case could crumble if you reach too high.

Words, words, mere words, no matter from the heart.

—Troilus and Cressida

What it means: The speaker keeps babbling on, but not saying anything useful. You are left to wonder whether the speaker even means any of what she is saying.

How to use it: When you want someone to "get real." You can also use it to point out that someone keeps talking around a subject but fails to get to the heart of the matter.

Be not afraid of greatness:
Some are born great,
Some achieve greatness,
And some have greatness thrust upon them.

—Twelfth Night

What it means: Don't be intimidated because you perceive someone else's stature as greater than your own. Alternatively, read this as "It's your time to shine. Don't worry about what advantages someone else has. You can do this."

How to use it: To remind yourself or someone else— perhaps a witness—to step forward with courage.

Have more than thou showest,
Speak less than thou knowest,
Lend less than thou owest.

— King Lear

What it means: Don't put all your cards on the table. Keep some knowledge, and some resources, in reserve.

How to use it: As a reminder not to gamble more than one can afford to lose in any negotiation or case.

The air-drawn dagger.

— Macbeth

What it means: Someone has the power to go in for the kill. Checkmate is at hand. Will the person with the upper hand use it?

How to use it: When someone has the power to finish off the opponent. Perhaps a fatal admission was just made that could seal the case. Can also be used to consider an ethical dilemma. You have come by knowledge fatal to your opponent's case, but you came by it accidentally, such as by a misdirected fax or e-mail. What will you do?

Life's but a walking shadow, a poor player
That struts and frets his hour upon the stage,
And then is heard no more; It is a tale
Told by an idiot, full of sound and fury,
Signifying nothing.

— Macbeth

What it means: Don't take yourself, or anyone else, too seriously. For better or for worse, this too shall pass.

How to use it: To remind yourself that most of what you do is going to be lost to the ages in a century, or even a year. Don't put too much importance on your daily activities.

41

Reputation is an idle and most false imposition;
Oft got without merit, and lost without deserving.

— Othello

What it means: Celebrity is fleeting. The most admired people are not necessarily those most deserving of admiration, and admiration is often lost for no good reason too.

How to use it: To remind yourself that you, and your opponent, are neither as great nor as bad as others are saying.

I *wear not*
My *dagger in my mouth.*

— *Cymbeline*

What it means: I don't seek to win by being the loudest or the most vulgar.

How to use it: To show an opponent, your client, or a jury that you're not one to scream and yell to win a case, but that you will win on merit without the drama.

What's past is prologue.

—The Tempest

What it means: History repeats itself.

How to use it: In court, to show (where permissible under the Rules of Evidence) that the opposing party has done this sort of thing before. Outside of court, you can use it to make the same point informally.

Chapter Two
The Game's Afoot

I see you stand like greyhounds in the slips,
Straining upon the start. The game's afoot. . .

—Henry V

Lawyers doing battle with each other. For litigators, there are few things more invigorating than waking up on the morning of a new trial day. The anticipation is often compared to a major-league athlete gearing up for the big game. In the single-minded focus of impending competition, ambition sometimes becomes indistinguishable from advocacy.

Shakespeare was a master at capturing the swelling excitement of a competitor who felt himself gaining the advantage. And yet, he was also circumspect—appearing to admonish the players not to lose sight of the purpose of the game, nor appear to be enjoying the circumstances too much.

Given the real stakes for the parties we represent, both the exhilaration of the challenge and the cautions from the Bard are worthy of review.

The play's the thing
Wherein I'll catch the conscience of the king.

— Hamlet

What it means: Hamlet is going to try to get the king to admit he killed Hamlet's father by writing and staging a fictional play that closely parallels the murder.

How to use it: In trying to get an opposing party to admit to something during cross examination, tell a hypothetical story that is very similar to your theory of the case. Perhaps change one key detail. It may be that the defendant cannot help but correct your one "faulty" detail, thereby admitting that the rest of your scenario is true.

47

Why may that not be the skull of a lawyer?
Where be his quiddities now, his quillets
His cases, his tenures and his tricks?

— Hamlet

What it means: How can that guy be a lawyer? He's not duplicitous or smarmy enough. What happened to all of his nastiness? (Note that in the play, this is literally a skull on a stick, not merely a metaphor.)

How to use it: Rhetorically, it can be used to show that the person you're talking about, whether he's a lawyer or some other person often looked at through a stereotypical lens, is in fact just a human being.

Alternatively, use this to show that in death, we are all the same. Ashes to ashes, dust to dust.

'Tis my vocation, Hal;
'tis no sin for a man to labour in his vocation.

— *King Henry IV*

What it means: I'm just doing my job—I didn't make the rules, but I do have to follow them.

How to use it: When someone asks how you can do what you do, have this handy answer ready.

I'll not budge an inch.

—The Taming of the Shrew

What it means: I am not going to relent on even the smallest part of my argument.

How to use it: In negotiations, or in a protracted court battle, use of this signals that you will not concede anything.

Fight till the last gasp.

— King Henry VI, Pt. I

What it means: Much like "I'll not budge an inch," but stronger—I will never give up this fight until I win or die trying.

How to use it: To signal to yourself, your opponent, or your client that you're not going to give up, no matter what. It's safe to say that the majority of lawyers go into court prepared to "fight till the last gasp."

I *will make a* Star Chamber *matter of it.*

—*The Merry Wives of Windsor*

What it means: I am going to make sure I win this, even if I have to railroad somebody in an unfair trial to do it. The Star Chamber was a Medieval English court that sat at the royal Palace of Westminster until its demise in 1641. The court basically existed to help those in power avoid conviction in the ordinary courts, and became a symbol of the corruption of the English monarchy.

How to use it: Sarcastically, to shame your opponent for over-reaching. This can be used any time your opponent threatens to reveal improperly prejudicial or irrelevant information in order to swing court or public opinion to his side, regardless of the weak merits of his case.

52

Chok'd with ambition of the meaner sort.

— Henry VI, Pt. 1

What it means: This guy, whether opposing counsel or opposing party, is so intent on winning at all costs that he doesn't care who he steps on to get what he wants. In fact, he may enjoy humiliating people. Think of the Ari Gold character played by actor Jeremy Piven in the HBO series "Entourage."

How to use it: Pointedly, to call out such a person—let the jury or the court know about the scorched-earth tactics your opponent is employing.

We *are* not *born* to *sue*, *but* to *command*.

— King Richard II

What it means: Law is a means of gaining power. We lawyers are not here just to file lawsuits like drones. We are here to make the world comply with our own vision of how things should be.

How to use it: Sarcastically, to call out an opponent who you believe is misusing the inherent power of the legal system to manipulate something to his own ends. You could also use it as a kind of rallying cry, to encourage yourself or your team members to use their legal skills to mold a more just and virtuous world and help advance the rule of law.

Delays have dangerous ends.

— Henry VI

What it means: Repeated continuances are threatening to weaken this case. In a nutshell: Justice delayed is often justice denied.

How to use it: To a judge when an opponent is asking for yet another delay, especially if you think they are simply stalling in hopes that a witness becomes unavailable or something equally damaging to your side happens in the interim.

I *perceive here a divided duty.*

—*Othello*

What it means: I think someone has a conflict of interest.

How to use it: When you are asking a court to consider whether your opponent has a conflict that should preclude him from continuing in the case. Alternatively, use it to chastise your people if they talk too much about how the firm will benefit from a case, as opposed to how the client will benefit.

I will speak daggers to her, but use none.

—Hamlet

What it means: I will speak harshly to this person to make my point, but I mean no real harm.

How to use it: To explain to a client or a protective judge that you may have to raise your voice a bit to a witness, but you're doing it for a reason and you promise not to cross the line.

The silence often of pure innocence
Persuades when speaking fails.

—The Winter's Tale

What it means: When you are accused of something so absurd as to be ridiculous, do not even justify it with a response. Sort of the polar opposite of the oft-quoted, "Methinks she doth protest too much."

How to use it: To explain why your client refuses to respond to something; a way of saying, "Look at the facts, then look at my client. Is this someone who would have done the ludicrous thing that the other side claims she did?" You can also use it to explain to a jury why your

58

client decided not to take the witness stand, if your strategy calls for you to explain your client's failure to testify. (Obviously, you're generally under no obligation to explain this, but sometimes you know that the jury is wondering and you decide to address the speculation.)

Virtue is bold, and goodness never fearful.

— Measure for Measure

What it means: When you know you're right, be courageous and unafraid to pursue justice. Right makes might.

How to use it: As a pep talk to remind yourself, your colleagues, or your client of the virtue of your cause.

Though this be madness, yet there is method in't.

—Hamlet

What it means: This may look like a crazy way to seek justice, but there are good reasons for all of this.

How to use it: To explain the vagaries of the court system to a client or other non-lawyer—to show that every seemingly pointless rule actually has a reasonable explanation.

Chapter Three
Witnesses and Other Fools

Be not thy tongue thine own shame's orator.

—A Comedy of Errors

Testimony: The Best and Worst Sort of Evidence.
Every litigator knows that you never ask a witness a question that you don't already know the answer to. And even with this precaution, witnesses manage to confound the court and muddy the lawyers' carefully laid plans more often than any of us cares to admit.

In less formal settings such as depositions or "conversations" with opposing parties—or the police—people seem to have an innate tendency to say too much. They trap themselves in a corner like novice chess players, leaving more experienced rivals to pounce on the smallest miscue.

Thus it has apparently always been, at least as far back as Shakespeare's time.

Gratiano speaks an infinite deal of nothing, more than any man in all Venice. His reasons are as two grains of wheat hidden in two bushels of chaff: You shall seek all day ere you find them, and when you have them, they are not worth the search.

—The Merchant of Venice

What it means: He talks a lot, but there's no substance to anything he says.

How to use it: To make the point that a witness is rambling on with explanation or excuses, but is not answering the core question.

She speaks, yet she says nothing.

— Romeo and Juliet

What it means: Similar to the previous quote from *The Merchant of Venice*—the witness is babbling, but not saying anything useful.

How to use it: To point out to the court or the jury that the witness isn't actually saying anything useful. Perhaps she is trying to avoid the question or talk around it.

The saying is true,
"The empty vessel makes the greatest sound."

— Henry V

What it means: Another variation on speaking, and yet saying nothing. The person with the most to say often has the least to contribute.

How to use it: To warn a jury that the witness who seems to know the most may not actually know anything, but may only be speculating.

Tempt not a desperate man.

— Romeo and Juliet

What it means: When someone is panicked or desperate, he or she will say or do almost anything.

How to use it: To point out that the witness may be tempted to "misremember" certain facts she is testifying about.

*A calendar, a calendar! Look in the almanack;
find out moonshine.*

— A Midsummer Night's Dream

What it means: Even the most mundane and obscure of facts can be checked or challenged, including whether or not there was a full moon on the night of the incident in question.

How to use it: To point out to a witness—perhaps during trial prep, if they're a friendly witness—that every detail counts and nothing should be said that the witness isn't certain of.

> In law, what plea so tainted and corrupt
> But being seasoned with gracious voice,
> Obscures the show of evil?

—*The Merchant of Venice*

What it means: Don't be fooled by how pleasant and reasonable this witness seems; his testimony obscures the evil he has done.

How to use it: To point out to a jury that just because the witness seems like a nice person doesn't mean that everything he says is true. Don't let him fool you.

*The seeming truth which cunning times put on
To entrap the wisest.*

—*The Merchant of Venice*

What it means: The explanation sounds reasonable on the surface, but the more you consider it, the less sense it makes.

How to use it: To remind a court that a witness' explanation may sound good, but still be false.

But *if it is a sin to covet honor,*
I am the most offending soul alive.

— Henry V

What it means: I always strive to do the right thing.

How to use it: Sardonically, to impeach a witness who insists that he always does what's right, no matter the consequences—especially where the evidence says otherwise.

Bait the hook well: This fish will bite.

— Much Ado about Nothing

What it means: This witness is about to step into a trap and doesn't know it.

How to use it: To counsel a colleague on how to impeach a witness: lay his foundation well, and the witness will practically impeach himself.

Not that I loved Caesar less,
but that I loved Rome more.

— Julius Caesar

What it means: An explanation of why a witness would seemingly do something not in his own or his friend's best interest. He is suggesting there was a higher interest to be served.

How to use it: To help your client testify to the reasons for his own behavior.

Cowards die many times before their deaths;
The valiant never taste of death but once.

—Julius Caesar

What it means: Those who do the wrong thing are always looking over their shoulders, waiting to be caught. Those who do the right thing never have to worry.

How to use it: To explain a witness' behavior. If the witness is on your side, emphasize the second part. If the witness is on the opposing side, emphasize the first part.

Always the dullness of the fool
Is the whetstone of the wits.

— As You Like It

What it means: The stupid things that dumb people do amuse smarter people.

How to use it: This could be used to explain a witness' behavior, such as why a police officer and his colleagues were making fun of a suspect. For example, "Dumb-criminal jokes help the cops blow off steam."

*The little foolery that wise men have makes
a great show.*

— As You Like It

What it means: When smart or powerful people do something dumb, people are interested and amused, sometimes disproportionately.

How to use it: To explain the great interest, perhaps more than is warranted, in some dumb thing a well-known person has done. Use this especially when the "foolishness" is ironic. For example, an absent-minded professor who studies minute details about obscure topics, but wears two different socks because he doesn't pay attention to his own dress.

I shall never be ware of mine own wit,
Till I break my shins against it.

— As You Like It

What it means: Why can't I learn to keep my mouth shut?

How to use it: This can be used as an admonishment to oneself, or to point out the foolishness of a witness. For example, "I may have been going a few miles over the speed limit, your Honor, but I wasn't doing 75 mph as the officer testified." Of course, with this, the witness has just admitted he was speeding. Verdict: Guilty.

Answer me in one word.

— *As You Like It*

What it means: Just answer the question. Do not embellish or explain.

How to use it: When prepping a witness, to remind her to make the questioner do the work. Just say yes or no—don't explain.

The fool doth think he is wise,
But the wise man knows himself to be a fool.

—*As You Like It*

What it means: The more you think you know, the dumber you really are, and vice versa.

How to use it: When a witness is showing that he clearly believes he's the smartest person in the room, and you prove him wrong, use this to sum up what just happened. Or, use it to warn your own witness not to be cocky.

Seems, Madam! Nay, it is: I know no "seems."

— Hamlet

What it means: Just the facts, ma'am. Tell me what you saw, not what you think was happening.

How to use it: To call out a witness who is embellishing her testimony with her own analysis.

The lady doth protest too much, methinks.

—Hamlet

What it means: The more she insists something is true, the less inclined I am to believe her. She wouldn't be so invested in having me believe this unless she was trying to fool me.

How to use it: To point out that a witness' testimony is perhaps a bit too pat. The more she proclaims certainty, the less convincing she sounds.

Do you think I am easier to be played than on a pipe?

—Hamlet

What it means: Who do you think you're kidding?

How to use it: When a witness is telling an obviously absurd story.

Assume a virtue, if you have it not.

— Hamlet

What it means: Fake it till you make it.

How to use it: To prep a reluctant witness: "Don't show that you're unsure. Be confident and people are more likely to believe you."

The jury, passing on the prisoner's life,
May in the sworn twelve have a thief or two
Guiltier than him they try.

— *Measure for Measure*

What it means: In Biblical terms, let he who is without sin cast the first stone. In modern courtroom terms, at least one or two of the jurors are bound to have a few skeletons in their own closets.

How to use it: In trying to habilitate a problematic witness, such as a co-conspirator or someone already convicted of something worse than what the present defendant is accused of, to remind the court that nobody's perfect.

He that is robb'd, not wanting what is stol'n,
Let him not know't and he's not robb'd at all.

— *Othello*

What it means: No harm, no foul.

How to use it: To make an analogy, whether serious or sarcastic, that if the victim was not actually injured, the defendant should not be found guilty or liable.

An *honorable murderer*, *if you will;*
For nought I did in hate, but all in honor.

— *Othello*

What it means: I killed him, but I had to.

How to use it: To show that the accused did the right thing, perhaps in self defense or defense of someone else. Or, conversely, to show that the defendant believes he did the honorable thing, so much so that he admits to doing it—but what he did is still illegal. We don't condone "an eye for an eye" in our legal system.

Mend your speech a little,
Lest you may mar your fortunes.

— *King Lear*

What it means: Be careful what you say or you could ruin this whole case.

How to use it: To warn a witness to say as little as possible, and be as clear as possible, so as not to put his foot in his mouth.

Keep a good tongue in your head.

—The Tempest

What it means: Don't lose your temper. Be concise, deliberate and calm when you speak.

How to use it: To warn your friendly witness during prep not to let his temper or his harsh tongue get the better of him.

Chapter Four
Lies, Liars, and Slander

For slander lives upon succession
Forever housed where it gets possession.

—A Comedy of Errors

The Opposite of Truth. For Shakespeare, nothing was worse than a lie. Such was his reverence for the truth that even when he has a character lie for a seemingly good reason, it almost always ends badly.

Among other things, the law is supposed to be about finding the truth. Our legal system was built on the premise that finding the truth is the first step in doing justice. Though it is easy to lose sight of this truth-seeking function of the law in modern day practice, it is an issue with which all lawyers wrestle.

There is no vice so simple but assumes
Some mark of virtue on its outward parts.

—The Merchant of Venice

What it means: Even though some good may come of something terrible, it's still terrible.

How to use it: When an opposing party or counsel is trying to downplay the seriousness of something bad that they are responsible for. (For example: "Sure, he lost a leg in the accident, but he met his wife in rehab, so it's not all bad!")

Like a fair house built upon another man's ground.

—The Merry Wives of Windsor

What it means: Taking credit for someone else's work.

How to use it: When someone fails to give credit where it is due, point it out with this handy quote.

Done to death by slanderous tongues.

— *Much Ado about Nothing*

What it means: Someone's reputation has been completely destroyed by lies told about him.

How to use it: To proclaim a client's innocence, particularly where false rumors abound. This quote could also be useful when a crime has received a large amount of pretrial press and has been tried in the papers, so to speak, and the defendant is widely considered guilty before any evidence is heard.

I'll starve err I'll rob a foot further.

— Henry IV

What it means: I will not continue this charade. I am finished with this dirty business.

How to use it: When you are withdrawing from a case or other situation because you believe your client isn't playing fair.

A politician . . . one that would circumvent God.

—Hamlet

What it means: Like a politician, you're always looking for a loophole to avoid doing the right thing.

How to use it: To call out a client who is asking you to help find a way around something that is legally required.

O, *what may man within him hide,*
Though angel on the outward side.

— Measure for Measure

What it means: Even some people who appear to be upstanding citizens have skeletons in their closets. Don't judge a book by its cover—even a pretty cover.

How to use it: When you need to show that someone is hiding dark secrets even though he appears to be just a nice, normal person.

Be *sure* of it; *give me the ocular proof.*

—*Othello*

What it means: Prove it. Show me the evidence.

How to use it: When you cannot take someone's word for something and need to see it for yourself; alternately, you could use it to introduce a dramatic piece of evidence.

No hinge nor loop to hang a doubt on.

— *Othello*

What it means: I cannot find any glitch in this person's story. He must be telling the truth.

How to use it: Use this to eloquently express your belief that someone's story is airtight.

> But this denoted a foregone conclusion.

> — *Othello*

What it means: You're assuming things that haven't yet been proven.

How to use it: To point out that someone has skipped a critical evidentiary step or glossed over something that needs to be addressed. You could also use it when someone attempts to drop a bombshell, but it turns out to be something that is already well known.

Time will unfold what plighted cunning hides;
Who covers faults, at last shame them derides.

— *King Lear*

What it means: The truth will come to light eventually, no matter how well you try to hide it. There is no such thing as the perfect crime.

How to use it: To make the point that someone who does something wrong, or illegal, will eventually get caught. The short-term reward is not worth the long-term damage.

The prince of darkness is a gentleman.

— King Lear

What it means: Even an evil person can pretend to be polite, but don't be fooled.

How to use it: To discourage a judge or jury from falling for a bad guy's pretense of being a nice guy.

Away, and mock the time with fairest show;
False face must hide what the false heart doth know.

— Macbeth

What it means: Keep a stiff upper lip. Don't let your weaknesses or your inner turmoil show. Put on a happy face.

How to use it: To remind yourself or your client to keep it together and not to let anyone know how you really feel. Alternatively, you can use this quote to impeach an opposing party's contention that some evidence shows his client did not appear worried or troubled in the time-frame right after he allegedly committed a crime or other bad act—demonstrate that he was just putting on a good show to hide what he did.

Slander,
Whose edge is sharper than the sword,
Whose tongue outvenoms all the worms of the Nile,
Whose breath rides on the posting winds
And doth belie
All corners of the world.

— Cymbeline

What it means: To slander someone is the most insidi-ous way to ruin him, because false rumors can be nearly impossible to correct once they're repeated enough.

How to use it: To show why falsely speaking ill of some-one to others and spreading rumors is as bad or worse

105

than assaulting them in some other way. This is another quote that can work well if you're defending someone who's been all over the news.

By telling of it,
Made such a sinner of his memory,
To credit his own lie.

—The Tempest

What it means: If you tell a lie often enough, even you will begin to believe it's true.

How to use it: To point out that just because a witness or opposing party claims to remember something a certain way does mean that's exactly how it happened; you can also use it to point out that someone is not only lying to others, but to himself as well.

Chapter Five
Mercy, Justice, and Truth

We cannot hold morality's strong hand.

—King John

The means and ends of the law. Shakespeare had a lot to say about the intersection of mercy and justice. At times he seemed to advocate the former as a means to the latter; in other places, he appears to admonish weak-willed authorities to teach someone a lesson rather than write off his sins. The one thing that seems clear from Shakespeare's writing is that he believed that mercy and justice ride hand-in-hand—and that it must always be so in a truly civilized society.

Shakespeare also clearly reveres truth. He seems to believe that there is a clear truth in every situation, and that, sooner or later, it will come to light.

Forbear to judge, for we are sinners all.

— Henry VI

What it means: Don't judge this person too harshly. You might have done the same thing in his shoes.

How to use it: As a plea for mercy to judge or jury.

Suspicion always haunts the guilty mind;
The thief doth fear each bush an officer.

— Henry VI

What it means: Sometimes the worst punishment is simply having to live with what you've done.

How to use it: To show that the person with the guilty mind will never be free of it, no matter his legal sentence.

Off *with his head!*

—Richard III

What it means: I've heard enough! Guilty!

How to use it: To chide those who would convict and try your client without hearing all the evidence. Using it in its straightforward meaning could backfire, echoes of the Queen of Hearts from *Alice and Wonderland*.

To unmask falsehood and bring truth to light.

—*The Rape of Lucrece*

What it means: There's more to this story than what you've heard.

How to use it: As a plea for the court to withhold judgment until your side of the story has been told.

114

Sweet mercy is nobility's true badge.

—Titus Andronicus

What it means: This is one of many places where Shakespeare calls on the powerful to be merciful to the less powerful. Here he is saying that to truly be worthy of respect, one must be willing to be merciful, not tyrannical.

How to use it: To remind a court that with the robe comes the duty to do justice, not merely to do the expedient thing.

And what makes robbers bold but too much lenity?

— Henry VI

What it means: Contrary to the spirit of the previous quote, this one basically says that if you go too easy on a wrong-doer, he will just do something worse the next time.

How to use it: As a prosecutor or plaintiff's attorney, to call upon the court to be firm in its verdict and sentence.

For we may pity, though not pardon thee.

— Comedy of Errors

What it means: We understand why you did it, and sympathize, but you still must be punished.

How to use it: When your opponent is calling for too much mercy—if they're subtly asking for jury nullification, respond that sympathy alone cannot guide the verdict.

And oftentimes excusing of a fault
Doth make the fault worse by the excuse.

— King John

What it means: Similar to the two previous items, this quote says that too much leniency leads to a sense of entitlement.

How to use it: To explain why a harsher punishment than the one the defense is requesting is warranted. For example, they may argue that it's too strict for the high school quarterback who got caught drinking to get suspended and possibly miss out on being seen by the college scouts. You argue that to excuse his misdeed will send the wrong message—to this kid and others coming up behind him.

Nothing emboldens sin so much as mercy.

—Timon of Athens

What it means: Yet another attempt by Shakespeare to warn against showing too much mercy when someone is not really repentant.

How to use it: To warn that letting someone off the hook will likely result in him committing even bigger misdeeds because he hasn't suffered consequences.

Virtue itself turns vice, being misapplied;
And vice some time's by action dignified.

— Romeo and Juliet

What it means: Nothing is all good or all bad. Every action must be viewed in context.

How to use it: To remind the jury or the court not to view the defendant's actions in a vacuum, but to place them in their proper context. For example: Man shoots dog = bad. Man shoots dog that is attacking his wife = good.

Banish plump Jack,
And banish all the world.

— Henry IV

What it means: If you're going to hold this small thing against this person, you should convict everybody in the world, because they have all done the same thing.

How to use it: To explain that not every misdeed calls for punishment.

The brain may devise laws for the blood,
But a hot temper leaps o're a cold decree.

—*The Merchant of Venice*

What it means: He knew right from wrong, but the heat of the moment overtook his senses.

How to use it: To argue that your client suffered temporary insanity due to the circumstances; for instance, if your client killed his wife's lover after finding his wife in bed with him.

To do a great right, do a little wrong.

—*The Merchant of Venice*

What it means: Civil disobedience should be seen as a virtue, not a vice.

How to use it: To make the point that while your client technically broke a law, his reason was valid and resulted in a greater good; for instance, if he broke into a building to rescue a child from harm.

Let the end try the man.

— Henry IV

What it means: Only god knows whether this person's deed should be punished.

How to use it: In a particularly thorny situation, where it's simply unclear whether the accused did the right thing or the wrong thing, you can use this quote to ask the court to err on the side of mercy.

Flat burglary as ever was committed.

— Much Ado about Nothing

What it means: If that's not a crime, then I don't know what one is.

How to use it: To discredit someone who is arguing they've done nothing wrong, when you believe the facts unequivocally show otherwise.

> So every bondman in his own hand bears
> The power to cancel his captivity.
>
> —Julius Caesar

What it means: This person could get himself out of trouble if only he'd tell what he knows.

How to use it: In a contempt situation in which someone refuses to testify, or when someone refuses to speak to authorities about what happened, recognizing that he will be punished as a co-conspirator for refusing to tell on his friends.

Some to the common pulpits and cry out,
"Liberty, freedom, and enfranchisement!"

—*Julius Caesar*

What it means: Another call from Shakespeare to commit civil disobedience where warranted.

How to use it: To show that an accused was trying to shed light on a problem, not merely committing a criminal act for his own benefit; for example, an activist who trespasses in order to stop an activity he believes to be detrimental to society or the environment.

127

It is not nor it cannot come to good.

—Hamlet

What it means: No matter how you look at this, it's bad.

How to use it: To show that there's no excuse for what someone has done; for instance, you cannot shoot the president of the logging company in an attempt to stop the cutting of trees.

> *'Tis in my memory lock'd,*
> *And you yourself shall keep the key of it.*

— Hamlet

What it means: I'll never say a word unless you give me permission to reveal what I know.

How to use it: To let someone, such as a client, know that you will never reveal what they have told you. It works as an elegant restatement of attorney-client privilege.

Murder most foul . . .

—Hamlet

What it means: A terrible thing.

How to use it: To explain to a court or jury, such as in an opening statement, that the evidence they will see is going to be extraordinarily gruesome.

> There is nothing either good or bad
> But thinking makes it so.

— Hamlet

What it means: Another call for context. Some things are not as bad as they seem; other things are not as good as they seem. It's all in the context. This quote is of particular relevance to lawyers, who generally build the narrative of their case in a way that casts the most favorable light possible on their clients.

How to use it: To ask a court to set aside preconceived notions or prejudices and make a reasoned decision. "Why do I believe this thing is so bad? I have been taught it's bad, but is it, really?"

131

I *must be cruel only to be kind.*

— Hamlet

What it means: I have to punish you to teach you to do the right thing.

How to use it: As an explanation for a punishment rendered; you may recall "this hurts me more than it hurts you" from your own childhood.

We *know what we are*
But *we know not what we may* be.

— Hamlet

What it means: Don't be too hard on this person. Who knows what he may turn out to be.

How to use it: A call for mercy, particularly for a young offender, or as a reminder that many great people had troubled childhoods before they straightened up.

And liberty plucks justice by the nose.

— *Measure for Measure*

What it means: To remain true to our ideals we must follow the law, even when the results may seem unjust.

How to use it: To remind a court that its allegiance must be to the law, even if it means freeing a clearly guilty man.

Some rise by sin, and some by virtue fall.

— Measure for Measure

What it means: Some people get to the top by shady dealings; others fail to get things done because they won't compromise their ideals.

How to use it: To point out that determining the "good guy" and the "bad guy" in a situation cannot be done by measuring results alone—you have to look at the parties' actions leading up to the dénouement.

Condemn the fault, and not the actor of it?

— *Measure for Measure*

What it means: Hate the sin, not the sinner. This person did a bad thing, but she is not a bad person as a result.

How to use it: In a plea for mercy, perhaps at sentencing—remind the court that this one deed does not make the accused irredeemable.

The law hath not been dead, though it hath slept.

— Measure for Measure

What it means: Justice has not been done up to now, but now it will be.

How to use it: To let someone know that although some wrong-doing has been allowed to go on far too long, it is now being stopped.

O! It is excellent to have a giant's strength,
But it is tyrannous to use it like a giant.

— *Measure for Measure*

What it means: Another of Shakespeare's admonishments to the powerful to temper their strength with mercy.

How to use it: As a means of saying, "Just because you *can* severely punish my client, that doesn't mean you should."

Truth is truth, to the end of reckoning.

— Measure for Measure

What it means: No matter how someone tries to hide it, the truth is always the truth.

How to use it: To remind someone that the truth can set you free, or it can get you in hot water, but it cannot be changed.

The robb'd that smiles steals something from the thief.

—*Othello*

What it means: In the vernacular: Don't let the turkeys get you down.

How to use it: As a reminder that how one reacts to a situation is as important as the situation itself.

This even-handed justice.

— Macbeth

What it means: The law treats everyone equally.

How to use it: To make the point that the law is the law, no matter the status of the person to whom it applies. Think of instances where the underdog has taken on a giant, like *Erin Brockovich*.

The attempt and not the deed confounds us.

— Macbeth

What it means: It's not the fact that he did it that's so awful—it's the reason he gives for doing it.

How to use it: As a way of acknowledging that sometimes the reasons given for actions don't make sense, or make the crime even worse than it appears on the surface; for example, the accused confessing that he killed the victim in an argument about a sandwich.

Out, damned spot! Out I say!

— Macbeth

What it means: This is Lady Macbeth's most famous line, where she shows that she has been driven mad by guilt over a murder. She scrubs obsessively, but still sees blood on her hands.

How to use it: To show a guilty conscience—that the accused did something, perhaps repeatedly, that shows he felt guilty.

Heaven is above all yet; there sits a judge
That no king can corrupt.

— Henry VIII

What it means: Someday, the accused will have to face the judgment of God.

How to use it: As a form of solace when you feel justice has been denied, especially if you think the court acted as it did for reasons other than the evidence presented; for instance, if a judge throws the book at an offender so as not to seem soft on crime, and not because the crime or criminal was particularly egregious.

Chapter Six
Our Noble Profession

*The first thing we do,
let's kill all the lawyers.*

—Henry VI

Lawyers' Views on the Law. The practice of law is more than a job to those who do it. Once you learn the peculiar blend of Latin, "spin," and double-speak known as Legalese, you never look at anything quite the same again. Just ask anyone who is *not* a lawyer for confirmation—we are a different species of neighbors, friends, parents, and co-workers.

The camaraderie of having survived law school and the bar exam imbues the profession with a sort of *Hotel California* quality: You can check out anytime you like, but you can never leave. Basically, once a lawyer, always a lawyer.

This last section of *Shakespeare for Lawyers* commiserates with and celebrates that fact. We leave it to you to decide just what each quote here means to you.

We few, we happy few, we band of brothers;
For he today that sheds his blood with me
Shall be my brother.

— Henry V

I am tied to the stake, and I must stand the course.

— King Lear

You taught me language; and my profit on't is
I know how to curse: the red plague rid you,
For learning me your language.

—The Tempest

Has this fellow no feeling of his business,
That he sings at grave-making?

—Hamlet

My near'st and dear'st enemy.

— King Henry IV

Good counselors lack no clients.

— Measure for Measure

There's divinity that shapes our ends,
Rough-hew them how we will.

—Hamlet

The painful warrior famoused for fight,
After a thousand victories, once foil'd,
Is from the books of honor razed quite,
And all the rest forgot for which he toil'd.

—Sonnet 25

Once more unto the breach, dear friends, once more.

— Henry V

We must not make a scarecrow of the law,
Setting it up to fear birds of prey,
And let it keep one shape, till custom make it
Their perch and not their terror.

— Measure for Measure

And do as adversaries do in law,
Strive mightily,
But eat and drink as friends.

—The Taming of the Shrew

About the Author

Margaret Graham Tebo, known as Meg to her family and friends, is a lawyer and a member of the Illinois and Missouri bars. She received her law degree *cum laude* from St. Louis University School of Law and her undergraduate degree in journalism from the University of Illinois at Urbana-Champaign. She is a former award-winning senior writer for the *ABA Journal,* the flagship magazine of the American Bar Association. Currently she teaches media law and other journalism courses at Columbia College Chicago, practices real estate law, and writes from her home in Chicago.